This book is
presented to:
Cecelia Fuhr

"Dad's
Secretaries"
From
Becky Coker
Debi Martuick
Sue Ashbeck
Deb Richter
Connie Bartelt
Nancy Conner
Annamarie Novak
Wendy Luppi
Deb Koenig
Kelly Cleinschmidt

Sept. 2000

Text Copyright © MCMXCII Paula Beth Sheedy
Art Copyright © MCMXCII Lucy Rigg
All rights reserved
Published by The C. R. Gibson Company
ISBN 0-8378-4141-0
GB 661

God Knows

By Paula Beth Sheedy
Illustrated by Lucy Rigg

R. Gibson Company, Norwalk, Connecticut 06856

God knows
all my secrets,

He sees
into my heart...

He knows the secrets
of the heart.

Psalms 44:21

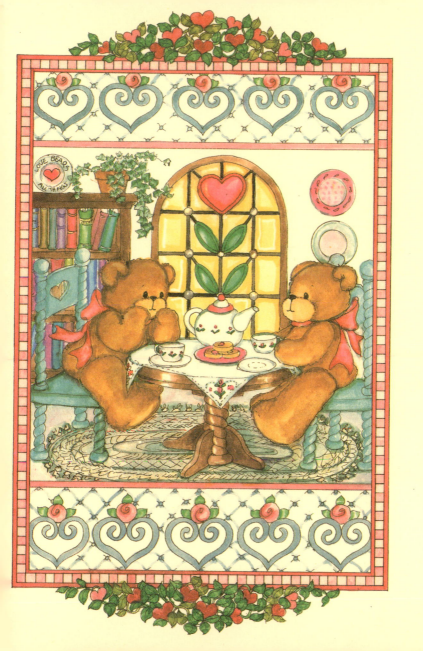

He knows
my birthday wishes,

He knows
my every thought.

May He give you
the desire of your heart.

Psalms 20:4

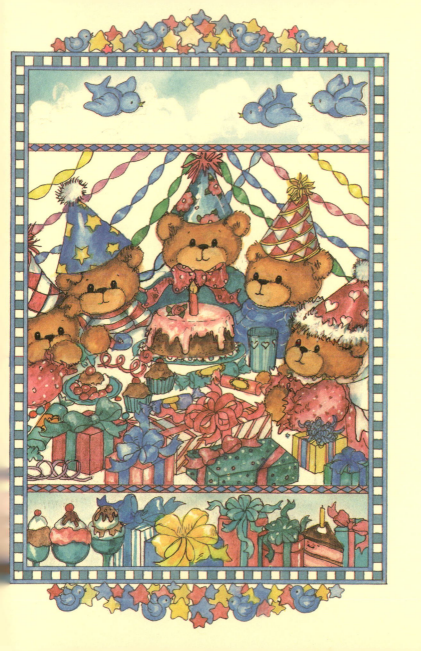

He's with me
when I'm sleeping,

He's there
when I'm awake...

When I awake,
I am still with You.
Psalms 139:18

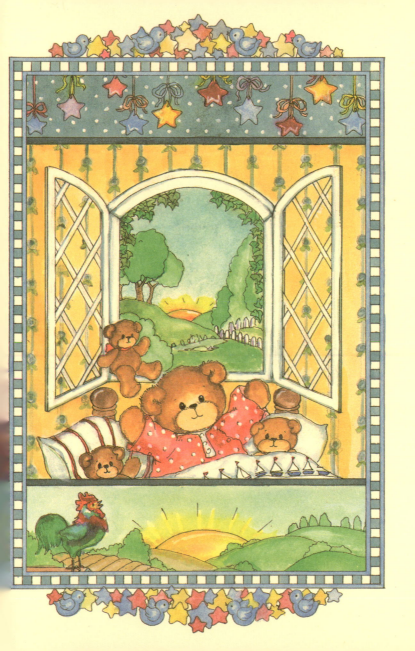

He's with me
on vacation

and every trip
I take.

I will be with you always.
Matthew 28:20

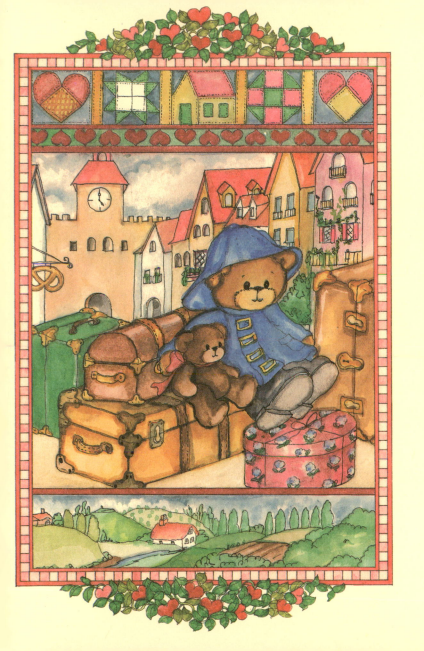

His banner over me is love.

He's just around the corner,

He's up above my head...

His banner over me is love.

Song of Songs 2:4

His banner over me is love.

I'm not afraid
of monsters,

God's underneath
my bed.

Do not fear
for I am with you.
Isaiah 41:10

I will be with you always.

He knows my name
and shoe size

and the color
of my hair.

Before I formed you
in the womb, I knew you.

Jeremiah 1:5

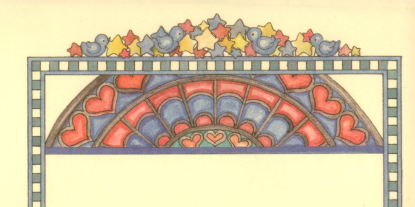

He knows that
I like chocolate,

and what
I like to wear...

Rejoice and be glad.
Matthew 5:12

He knows when
I've been bad or good,

He knows
how hard I've tried.

Whatever you do,
work at it with all your heart.
Colossians 3:23

NO
FISHING

He knows just how
sad I was

the day
my goldfish died.

He heals the brokenhearted.
Psalms 147:3

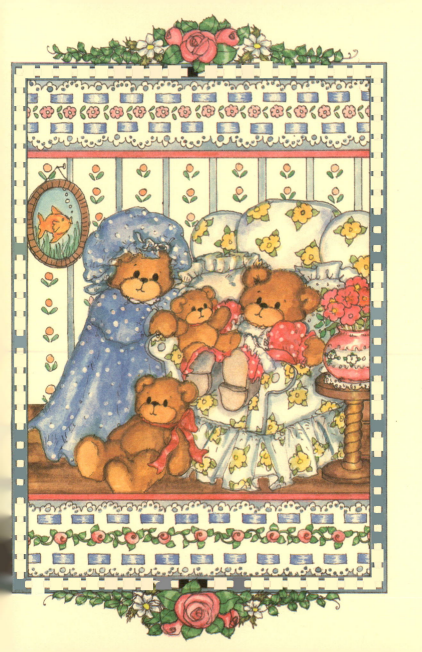

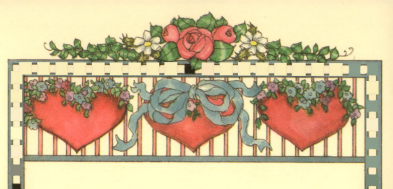

He's with me
when I'm lonely,

He's with me
when I'm blue...

The earth is full of
His unfailing love.
Psalms 33:5

God is love.
1 John 4:8

He knows who
I'll grow up to be,

and when
I'll marry, too.

For I know the plans
I have for you.
Jeremiah 29:11

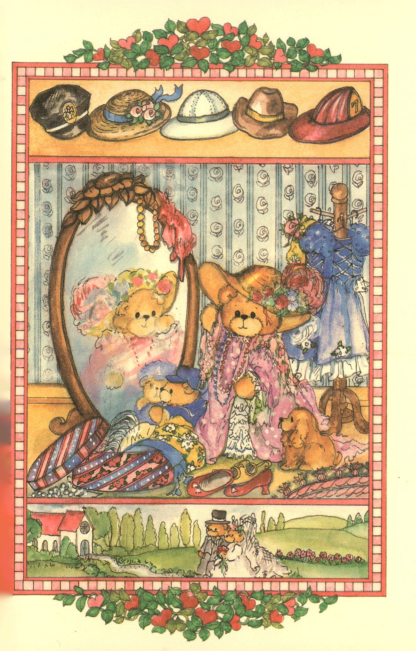

He knows my tears
and all my fears

and how happy
I can be...

He delivered me
from all my fears.
Psalms 34:4

That's the God
that I know...

You will fill me with joy
in your presence.

Psalms 16:11

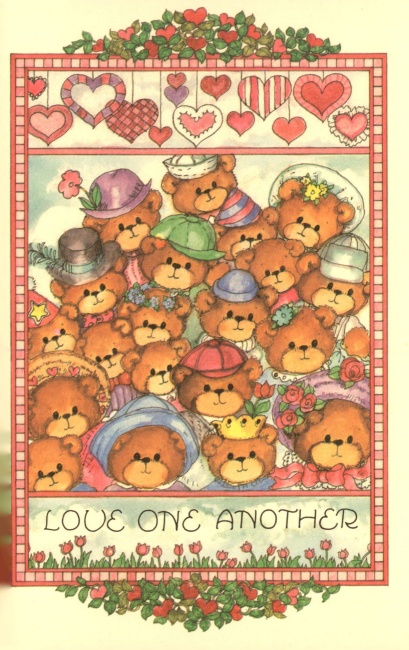

LOVE ONE ANOTHER

and I know
God knows me!

I have engraved you
on the palms of My hands.

Isaiah 49:16

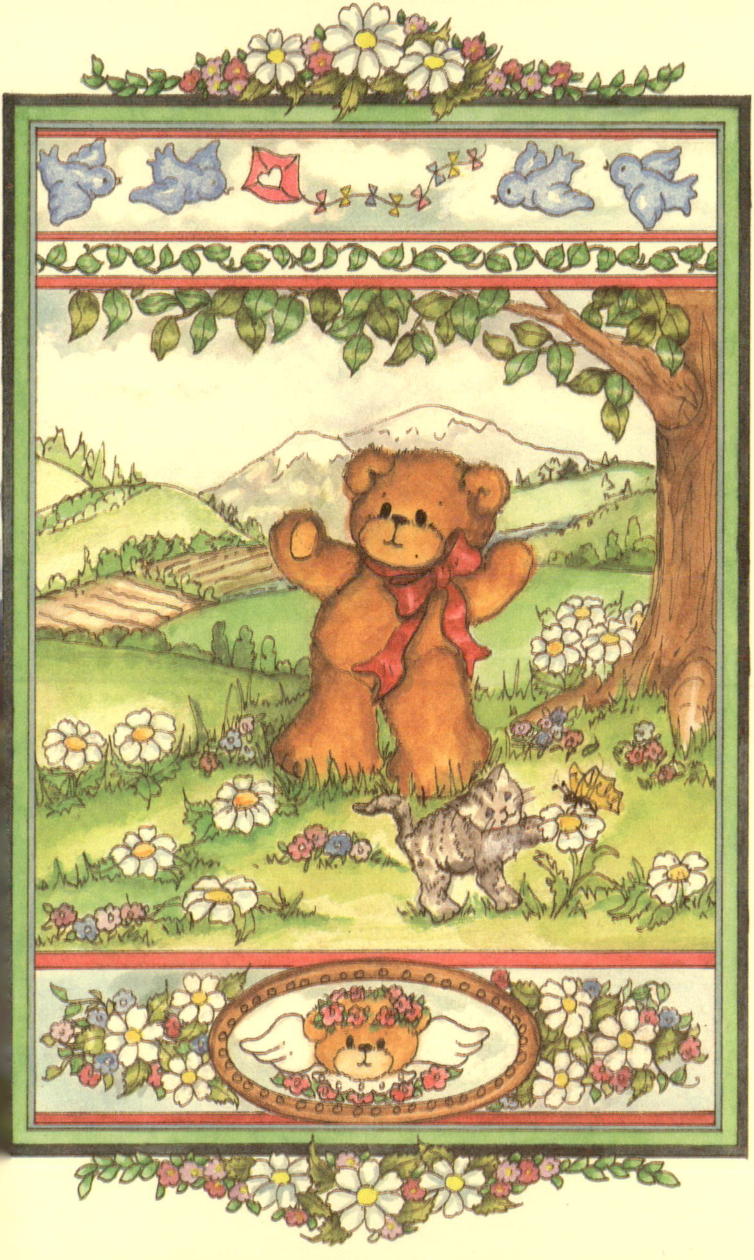

Bible Verses to Remember

The Lord is good
and His love endures forever.

Psalms 100:5

God is love.

1 John 4:8

A friend loves at all times.

Proverbs 17:17

Rejoice and be glad.

Matthew 5:12

Let us love one another,
for love comes from God.

1 John 4:7

My Favorite Verse